Grades 3–6

Artie Almeida
ADVENTURES
WITH THE
ORCHESTRA

A complete instructional unit to bring the orchestra to your students

HERITAGE MUSIC PRESS
A Lorenz Company • www.lorenz.com

Editor: Erika Popp
Cover Art and Book Design: Patti Jeffers

Heritage Music Press
A division of The Lorenz Corporation
P.O. Box 802
Dayton, OH 45401
www.lorenz.com

Printed in the United States of America.

ISBN: 978-0-7877-3338-4

©2016 Heritage Music Press, a division of The Lorenz Corporation, and its licensors. All rights reserved.

Permission to photocopy the manipulatives and worksheets included in this product is hereby granted to one teacher as part of the purchase price. This permission may not be transferred, sold, or given to any additional or subsequent user of this product. Thank you for respecting copyright law.

MW01133147

CONTENTS

Learn

Review

Listen

Explore

WELCOME!

For many years, teachers across the country and around the world have been inspired by the innovative and creative lessons cultivated in Artie Almeida's Florida classroom. In one of her earliest published resources, Dr. Almeida packaged several ideas for learning about the orchestra into a complete unit designed to thoroughly explore the instruments, vocabulary, and enjoyment of the symphony orchestra. Advances in technology have made it possible to bring you that same unit with many additional tools to make implementing every activity as simple as possible. Plus, we've added some of Artie's signature lessons designed to expose children to classical music in a meaningful way, using guided listening and WebVisits.

Our goal is to save you valuable planning time, so that you can focus on your students. The enclosed CD has a variety of teaching tools to complement each lesson plan in this book. We hope you find everything you need to give the children in your care a rigorous introduction to one of music's longstanding traditions—the incredible symphony orchestra.

About the CD

The CD in this book contains many types of files. Use any audio player to play the recordings. Open the CD with a computer to access the other types of files. You may need to install a PDF reader such as Adobe Acrobat to view PDF files. Visit *get.adobe.com/reader* for more information and a free download.

Finding Great Recordings

This book also has a companion website, located at **http://music4you.lorenz.com/orchestra.html**. Through this portal, you can access great performances of the classical music referenced in this book. They are available for purchase from NAXOS and its affiliate labels, and most can be downloaded or streamed. It is our hope that this resource helps you to find high-quality recordings to use in your classroom, without spending your valuable planning time searching for the best one.

BUILDING A LISTENING LIBRARY

The pieces listed below are very accessible and appealing to young students. Choose pieces from this list to use as entrance and exit music for your lessons, and seek out other opportunities to familiarize your students with these great compositions. You could feature one piece each week as the opening music for your school's television news broadcast (play the same piece each day of the week), or on the school's announcements. Use very brief excerpts to make this experience positive.

Consider creating listening maps for your favorite pieces, or using props to activate the experience. Props could include ribbon streamers, scarves, a parachute, beanbags, rhythm instruments, hula hoops, etc.

Leroy Anderson
Bugler's Holiday
The Syncopated Clock

Ludwig van Beethoven
Symphony #5 in C Minor, Op. 67, First Movement
Symphony #9 in D Minor, Op. 125, Fourth Movement

George Bizet
Toreador Song (from *Carmen*)

Johannes Brahms
Hungarian Dance #5

Aaron Copland
Hoe-Down (from *Rodeo*)

Patrick Doyle
The Quidditch World Cup

Michael Giacchino
Jurassic World

Morton Gould
American Salute

Percy Grainger
Children's March: Over the Hills and Far Away

Harry Gregson-Williams
Chronicles of Narnia

Edvard Grieg
In the Hall of the Mountain King (from *Peer Gynt Suite*)

George Frederic Handel
Royal Fireworks Music

Franz Joseph Haydn
Symphony No. 94 "Surprise" in G Major

Gustav Holst
Jupiter (from *The Planets*)

Aram Khachaturian
Sabre Dance (from *Gayane*)

Zoltán Kodály
The Viennese Clock (from *Háry János Suite*)

Wolfgang Amadeus Mozart
Eine Kleine Nachtmusik

Modest Mussorgsky, orch. Ravel
Ballet of the Unhatched Chicks (from *Pictures at an Exhibition*)
Great Gate of Kiev (from *Pictures at an Exhibition*)

Jacques Offenbach
Can Can (from Gaité Parisienne)

Nikolai Rimsky-Korsakov
Flight of the Bumblebee (from *Tale of Tsar Saltan Suite*)

Gioachino Rossini
William Tell Overture

Alan Silvestri
Back to the Future

Johann Strauss, Sr.
Radetsky March

Pyotr Ilyich Tchaikovsky
Trepak "Russian Dance" (from *The Nutcracker Suite*)
March (from *The Nutcracker Suite*)

John Williams
E.T. the Extra-Terrestrial Main Theme
Harry's Wondrous World
Hedwig's Theme
Raiders of the Lost Ark
Star Wars Main Theme

Extension Activity

Encourage students to listen for an orchestra in the soundtracks to their favorite movies. Play some powerful soundtrack music and ask the children to imagine how bland and unexciting the movie would be without that great orchestral music present. Can they imagine their favorite movie without its soundtrack?

Visit **http://music4you.lorenz.com/orchestra.html** to find recordings of the music **on this list.**

INTRODUCING ORCHESTRA VOCABULARY

Materials
- Orchestra Flashcards (CD)
- Word Scramble (page 14)
- Orchestra Vocabulary Assessment (page 16)
- Matching Terms Challenge (page 15)

Objective: Students will discuss and define orchestra vocabulary words.

For your convenience, you can either copy student pages directly from this book, or print them from the CD.

Before You Begin
Print the orchestra flashcards (front and back) in color or black and white. For extra durability, print them on cardstock and laminate them.

Directions
1. Play an exciting piece of orchestral music as your students enter the classroom. Visit **http://music4you.lorenz.com/orchestra.html** to download or stream Artie Almeida's recommended recordings.

2. Display an orchestra flash card.

3. Call on a student to read the word. Assist with pronunciation if necessary.

4. Read the definition on the back of the card. Discuss. Invite students to share what they already know about the vocabulary words.

5. Continue in this manner with the remaining flash cards.

After you've introduced all of the vocabulary words, use these variations to reinforce your students' knowledge:

1. Show each card and ask a student to define the vocabulary word.

2. Read the definition and choose a child to name the word that was defined.

3. Use the Orchestra Word Scramble to review vocabulary and help students to remember the words.

Assessment
1. Use the fill-in-the-blank Orchestra Vocabulary Assessment to review the terms, or as an informal assessment piece.

2. For a more formal assessment, perhaps at the end of your orchestra unit, use the Matching Terms Challenge.

Come back to the instrument flash cards as many times as you like over the course of your unit, using them to reinforce students' understanding of the vocabulary terms.

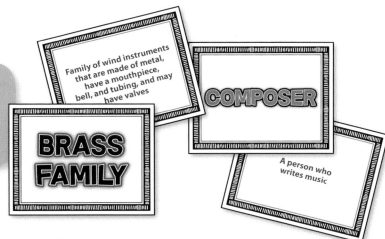

ORCHESTRA CONCENTRATION

Materials
• Orchestra Concentration Cards (CD)

Objective: Students will identify and define orchestra vocabulary words.

Before You Begin
Print the Orchestra Concentration Cards on both sides, so that each card has the Orchestra Concentration logo on one side and a word or definition on the other side. For extra durability, you could print them on cardstock and laminate them.

Directions
1. Play an exciting piece of orchestral music as your students enter the classroom. Visit **http://music4you.lorenz.com/orchestra.html** to download or stream Artie Almeida's recommended recordings.

2. Place the *Orchestra Concentration* cards face down on the classroom floor in four rows of five cards each (see diagram below). Position students around the cards, on the floor or in chairs, so that everyone can see each card.

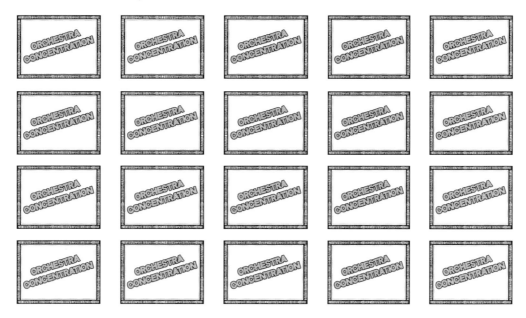

3. Divide students into two teams.

4. A student from Team One chooses two cards to turn over. If they are a match (orchestra vocabulary word and correct definition) the team scores a point. If the cards do not match, they should be turned back over.

5. A player from Team Two chooses two cards and tries to make a match.

6. Play proceeds in this manner until only two cards are left on the floor. The teacher then picks up the two remaining cards and displays, as well as reads aloud, the card that contains the definition. The student must state the correct vocabulary word, earning two points since it's more difficult. If this student chooses an incorrect word, the other team gets a chance to earn the two points.

GAME ON!

Use these games anytime to reinforce orchestra knowledge in an exciting way.

Twenty Questions (almost!)

One child stands in front of the class with a sign taped to his/her back that names an instrument. Only the student with the sign (and the teacher) knows what the instrument is. Students in class are allowed to ask yes or no questions to identify the instrument. The teacher stands out *behind* the other students, so the child with the sign can see the teacher. This way the teacher can help the child standing up front give the correct answers to the questions, with subtle head motions if necessary. The class member who guesses the answer is the next person up front.

On another day, reverse the process with the class knowing the instrument and the child in front asking questions to determine the answer. For example, the child might ask, "Am I in the brass family?" or "Do I use a reed?"

Four Corners Game

Label the four corners of the room with an instrument family sign – perhaps displayed on music stands or the backs of four chairs. I use *Brass Boulevard, String Street, Woodwind Way and Percussion Parkway*.

Make a square-shaped "mush pot" in the center of the room with surveyor's tape. Not only will this be the "mush pot" but it will also create a nice square "walkway" outside of the mush pot for the children to use.

Use the CD accompanying this book as a playlist and add in some of your favorite orchestra or band works. I love to intersperse great movie themes into the game as well. All students walk around the "road" with a piece of instrumental music playing. When the music stops all students must sit in the instrument family corner *nearest them*. (Be sure they understand this direction because in some Physical Education classes children are allowed to run to the corner of their choice.) Play an instrument clip (or an instrument *family* clip) and all students in that corner are out. *Mush! Mush! Mush!* To the mush pot they go.

Another option is to pull an instrument name or picture out of a bag to determine which students will be out. The winner is the "last man standing." I give reward stickers or first choice at instruments to the winner, although since it is just a game of chance, no rewards are necessary.

As the game is progressing, it is fun to ask the children in the mush pot to predict who will win. This keeps them engaged and enjoying themselves.

Scrambled!

Divide the class into two or three teams, seated "train-style" in long rows facing the front of the room. Prepare flash cards with scrambled instrument names and orchestra vocabulary words to be defined. (Some of your cards could be the *definition* of the vocabulary word and the children must name the word).

Provide the first child in each row with an audible answer-responder of some kind, such as a desk bell to strike or a hand bell to ring. My kiddos enjoy standing behind a tubano with a mallet and striking the drum when they know the answer. Children are to play the instrument *as soon as they think they know the correct answer, but not beforehand.* Make sure the first two children are ready with their responders, then choose a card to display. The first child to sound their instrument gets a chance to name the scrambled instrument or define the orchestra vocabulary word. If they are correct, their team gets a point, but if they are incorrect, the other child gets a chance to "steal the point." If the second child (player for team 2) does not know the answer, both children move to the back of the line and the next two players come forward to the audible responders for another round of play.

Consider using two different colors of paper for the two categories of cards. Print the answer lightly on the back of each flash card to make this game easy for a substitute teacher to use.

OUCRCDOTN

NTCLRAIE

A person who directs a band, orchestra, or choir

INSTRUMENT FAMILIES
Sorting Boards

Materials
- Activity board for each student (CD)
- Instrument picture sheet for each student (CD)
- Plastic storage bag for each student
- Listening excerpts (CD)
- Building a Listening Library (page 4)

Objective: Students will be able to describe the characteristics of each instrument family in the orchestra and identify the families by their sound.

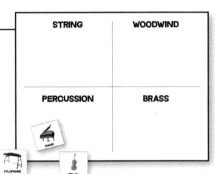

Before You Begin

The first time you do this activity, have students help create a set of activity boards and instrument pieces. Print and give an activity board and instrument picture sheet to each student, along with a plastic bag and scissors. Have students cut apart the instrument pieces and put them in the bag. Another option is to ask a parent volunteer to help you prepare the instrument picture packages. Both the Sorting Boards and Instrument Picture Sheets should be laminated for durability. Prepare a few extra instrument picture pages to use if individual pieces get lost.

Directions:

1. Play an exciting piece of orchestral music as your students enter the classroom. See page 4 for suggestions, or visit **http://music4you.lorenz.com/orchestra.html** to download or stream Artie Almeida's recommended recordings.

2. Distribute activity boards and bags of instrument pictures while an exciting piece of orchestral music plays in the background. (See page 4 for suggestions.)

3. Ask students to place their instrument picture pieces around the perimeter of their activity board. They should be able to see all of the pieces, but nothing should be placed on the sorting board itself.

4. Spend a few moments discussing the characteristics of human families. Ask students if any of their family members have physical characteristics in common. Perhaps everyone in a family is tall, has brown hair, blue eyes, etc.

5. Before beginning the listening portion of the activity, call on individual children to describe the characteristics of each instrument family, one at a time. Refer to the *Orchestra Flash Cards* for this information.

6. Begin the activity by playing Track 1 on the CD. Call on a student to name the family of instruments being played. When the correct answer is obtained (brass family) ask students to find all of the pictures of brass instruments and place them into the square on their board labeled "Brass Family." If they are struggling, give clues such as "There are four brass instrument pictures." If the music finishes before students have placed their pieces, replay the excerpt on the CD.

Track	Answer
1-2	Brass Family
3-4	String Family
5-6	Woodwind Family
7-8	Percussion Family

7. When students are finished with this task, discuss each of the instruments placed in the box. Call on students to name each instrument.

8. Challenge the students by asking them to place the instruments in high-to-low order (trumpet, French horn, trombone, tuba).

9. Continue the activity by playing an excerpt of another instrument family. Track 3 is the string family, but you may present the families in any order you wish. It will make the activity more challenging if you do not play the tracks in the same order as the boxes are listed on the activity boards.

10. As you present the remaining three families in the same way, extend students' knowledge with these challenges:

    a. After naming the string Instruments, instruct the students to place the four core instruments in high-to-low order (violin, viola, cello, string bass).

    b. Ask students to name string instruments that are used in styles of music other than classical. Some examples may be guitar, autoharp, dulcimer, mandolin, electric bass, etc. Discuss when each instrument may be used.

    c. After identifying the woodwind instruments (Track 5), ask students to name the two single reed instruments (clarinet, saxophone), and the two double reed instruments (oboe, bassoon).

    d. Ask students to name the highest (piccolo/flute) and the lowest (bassoon/contrabassoon) members of the woodwind family.

    e. Have students guess which instrument is used the least in the orchestra. You can guide them to the answer (saxophone) by sharing that this instrument was invented in the 1840s, after much of the orchestral repertoire was written.

    f. Ask students why the saxophone is a member of the woodwind family, rather than the brass family (it uses a reed). Discuss how Adolphe Sax envisioned his creation to be a bridge between the brass and woodwind families, so he endowed it with some characteristics of each. It includes many keys to help with fast technical passages that woodwind players see frequently, but is made of brass with a conical bore and upright bell to project strongly like a brass instrument.

    g. Listen to the first percussion instrument excerpt (Track 7) and ask students to name percussion instruments that have membranes or skins (snare drum, timpani), and percussion instruments whose sound is generated by wood or by metal (xylophone, cymbals, chimes). Move on to CD Track 8 to allow the children to hear and identify different percussion timbres.

    h. Ask students to name the percussion instrument that has strings (piano). Describe the piano action of a hammer striking a string, thus making the piano a percussion instrument.

11. End the lesson by asking students to describe the difference between a band and an orchestra. If necessary, give them the hint that the number of families involved is the difference. (band = brass, woodwind, percussion) (orchestra = string, brass, woodwind, percussion)

12. Discuss how the string family is the most plentiful in an orchestra with up to 30 or more members, compared to approximately 8 woodwinds, 9 brasses, and 3 or 4 percussionists.

13. Play a piece of exciting orchestral music (see page 4 for suggestions) as students pass in their activity boards and instrument picture pieces.

CLIP THE INSTRUMENT

Materials
- Clip the Instrument Boards for each student (CD)
- Clothespins for each student (optional)
- Clip the Instrument Clues (page 13)
- Listening excerpts (CD)

Objective: Students will identify instruments in the orchestra by their characteristics and by their sound.

Before You Begin:
Print the Clip the Instrument Boards. Use cardstock if possible. Then have students decorate and cut them out. At this point, you could collect the boards and laminate them, making them useful for longer.

Directions:
1. Play an exciting piece of orchestral music as your students enter the classroom. See page 4 for suggestions, or visit **http://music4you.lorenz.com/orchestra.html** to download or stream Artie Almeida's recommended recordings.

2. Read the clues on the next page, asking students to identify the instrument you describe by clipping their clothespin to the instrument. If you don't want to use clothespins, you can have students indicate each instrument by touching it between their thumb and index finger.

3. As you play, repeat instruments that students struggle to identify. You can make up your own clues to adapt the game more specifically to your own students. Continue this step until most students can identify all of the instruments quickly.

4. Use the CD to play listening excerpts of each instrument and ask students to identify the instrument they hear.

CD Track	Answer	CD Track	Answer
9	trombone	18	string bass
10	violin	19	oboe
11	bassoon	20	French horn
12	flute	21	harp
13	timpani	22	saxophone
14	cello	23	viola
15	trumpet	24	xylophone
16	clarinet	25	tuba
17	snare drum	26	piano

CLIP THE INSTRUMENT
Teacher Script

1. Clip a brass instrument that uses a slide. *trombone*

2. Clip the highest sounding member of the orchestral string family. *violin*

3. Clip a woodwind instrument that uses a double reed and bocal, the short pipe into which the reed fits. *bassoon*

4. Clip the highest sounding member of the Woodwind Family. The modern version is made of metal, but earlier versions were made of wood, ceramic, and even bone. *flute* (You may also wish to discuss that the piccolo is an even higher version of this instrument.)

5. Clip a percussion instrument whose nickname is kettle drums. They look like large copper kettles. *timpani*

6. Clip a string instrument that is rather large, with a peg that touches the floor and helps to hold the instrument. Players sit in a chair to play this instrument. *cello*

7. Clip the highest sounding brass instrument. *trumpet*

8. Clip a single reed instrument that is made of wood. *clarinet*

9. Clip a percussion instrument that has a membrane on the top and the bottom, as well as thin metal strips that vibrate against the bottom membrane, creating its unique sound. *snare drum*

10. Clip a large string instrument that has a very low sound, four strings and a short peg, upon which it stands. The player must stand, or sit on a tall stool, to play this instrument. *string bass*

11. Clip a small double reed instrument. *oboe*

12. Clip a brass instrument that is designed in a circular shape. It has three valves, which are pressed with the player's left hand. If this instrument were straightened, the tubing would be over eleven feet long! *French horn*

13. Clip a large string instrument that contains many strings, as well as numerous foot pedals. *harp*

14. Clip a woodwind instrument that uses a single reed, but is made of brass. *saxophone*

15. Clip a string instrument that resembles a violin, but is slightly larger, therefore lower in pitch. *viola*

16. Clip a percussion instrument that is constructed of tuned wooden bars. *xylophone*

17. Clip the lowest sounding member of the brass family. *tuba*

ORCHESTRA WORD SCRAMBLE

Directions: Unscramble each word to find the important vocabulary words of the orchestra.

1. (TRERCCEAOMTSN)

_ _ _ _ _ _ _ _ _ _ _ _

2. (RSASB)

_ _ _ _ _

3. (PAMRWU)

_ _ _ _ _ _

4. (CSONSIERPU)

_ _ _ _ _ _ _ _ _ _

5. (PSCMOERO)

_ _ _ _ _ _ _ _

6. (DWWIODON)

_ _ _ _ _ _ _ _

7. (GIUTNN)

_ _ _ _ _ _

8. (OUCRCDOTN)

_ _ _ _ _ _ _ _ _

9. (CREENO)

_ _ _ _ _ _

10. (TRSGNI)

_ _ _ _ _ _

The original purchaser of *Adventures with the Orchestra* has permission to reproduce this page for use in his or her classroom.
©2016 Heritage Music Press, a division of The Lorenz Corporation. All rights reserved. www.lorenz.com

Name: _____ Classroom Teacher: _____ Date: _____

MATCHING TERMS CHALLENGE

Directions: Match each vocabulary word on the left side with its definition on the right side. Draw a line to connect the word and the definition.

composer

Family of wind instruments that are made of metal, have a mouthpiece, bell, and tubing, and may have valves

concertmaster

A person who writes music

brass

The principal violin in an orchestra, who leads the violin section and plays all the solos

percussion

A person who directs a band, orchestra, or choir

conductor

A piece played after the final concert selection, due to the audience demand

warm-up

Instruments you hit, shake, or scrape to play

woodwinds

Instruments with strings that can be plucked, strummed, or bowed

encore

When orchestra members all play the same note before the concert begins, in order to sound good together

tuning

The time before the concert when each musician spends some time playing music of his or her choice

strings

Wind instruments made of wood or metal which often use a reed

The original purchaser of *Adventures with the Orchestra* has permission to reproduce this page for use in his or her classroom.
©2016 Heritage Music Press, a division of The Lorenz Corporation. All rights reserved. www.lorenz.com

Name: _____ Classroom Teacher: _____ Date: _____

ORCHESTRA VOCABULARY ASSESSMENT
Directions: Fill in each blank with the correct orchestra vocabulary word.

1. The _____ family of wind instruments are made of metal, have a mouthpiece, bell, and tubing, and may have valves.

2. A _____ is a person who writes music.

3. The principal violin in an orchestra, who leads the violin section and plays all the solos, is called the _____ .

4. A _____ is a person who directs a band, orchestra, or choir.

5. An _____ is a piece played after the final concert selection, due to audience demand.

6. Instruments you hit, shake, or scrape to play are in the _____ family.

7. Instruments with strings, that can be plucked, strummed, or bowed, are members of the _____ family.

8. A process in which orchestra members all play the same note before the concert begins, so that their instruments sound good together, is called _____ .

9. Before the concert, each musician spends some time playing music of his or her choice. This is called the _____ time.

10. Wind instruments made of wood or metal, which often use a reed, are part of the _____ family.

The original purchaser of *Adventures with the Orchestra* has permission to reproduce this page for use in his or her classroom.
©2016 Heritage Music Press, a division of The Lorenz Corporation. All rights reserved. www.lorenz.com

Name: _____   Classroom Teacher: _____   Date: _____

INSTRUMENT FAMILY WORD SEARCH
Directions: Using a highlighter or a pencil, identify the instrument names in each grid.

BRASS

```
M U I N O H P U E T
S O U S A P H O N E
C Y E W N W P A H G
V G T R O M B O N E
U Z D E X X Z L M K
K U T E N R O C G H
T E P M U R T A C M
F R E N C H H O R N
A A J G O L C T U K
P E B N Q T U B A S
```

TRUMPET   TROMBONE   TUBA   SOUSAPHONE
EUPHONIUM   FRENCH HORN   CORNET

WOODWINDS

```
A B A S S O O N S K
O L O C C I P U U R
E A U B Q O Z M E S
Y W P W B C J C J D
X E N O H P O X A S
I S E P T R A U H F
G J F A D U X M R L
X E A E Q M W U P U
B M R F R O Z K P T
C L A R I N E T A E
```

FLUTE   PICCOLO   CLARINET   RECORDER
SAXOPHONE   BASSOON   OBOE

STRINGS

```
P Q H A R P P L U G
M N K K L A F R N U
T B A N J O U C R I
G J M B B S I Q K T
T L M D M M U V N A
N C Z S L V Y E Y R
T E O A V A L H Y N
O L L E C I P I G D
S T R I N G B A S S
N K N I L O I V Y K
```

VIOLIN   VIOLA   CELLO   STRING BASS
HARP   GUITAR   BANJO

PERCUSSION

```
I T Y P J S M E A Y
Z I M H W E U N Q E
E M U J T M R O T N
J P R F G I D H R S
P A D F N H S P I L
I N E L O C S O A A
A I R C G Z A L N B
N Z A K Z L B Y G M
O C N F C F J X L Y
I Z S J P J C R E C
```

SNARE DRUM   BASS DRUM   GONG   CYMBALS
CHIMES   TRIANGLE   XYLOPHONE   TIMPANI   PIANO

The original purchaser of *Adventures with the Orchestra* has permission to reproduce this page for use in his or her classroom.
©2016 Heritage Music Press, a division of The Lorenz Corporation. All rights reserved. www.lorenz.com

Name: _____ Classroom Teacher: _____ Date: _____

DO YOU KNOW YOUR NEIGHBORS?

Color each instrument circle to match its family and draw a line from the instrument to the correct house.

Brass = Red **Woodwind = Blue** **String = Orange** **Percussion = Green**

STRING STREET

violin

snare drum

flute

BRASS BOULEVARD

viola

piccolo

saxophone

cymbals

trumpet

french horn

string bass

clarinet

harp

timpani

cello

bassoon

bass drum

chimes

glockenspiel

trombone

xylophone

gong

tuba

guitar

piano

PERCUSSION PARKWAY

WOODWIND WAY

oboe

euphonium

The original purchaser of *Adventures with the Orchestra* has permission to reproduce this page for use in his or her classroom.
©2016 Heritage Music Press, a division of The Lorenz Corporation. All rights reserved. www.lorenz.com

Name: _____   Classroom Teacher: _____   Date: _____

INSTRUMENT FAMILIES: SHOW WHAT YOU KNOW!
The instruments of the orchestra are listed in the Word Bank below.
Write each instrument's name in the correct instrument family section.

Word Bank

trumpet	oboe	cymbals	French horn	trombone
bass drum	viola	string bass	clarinet	timpani
cello	bassoon	euphonium	harp	violin
xylophone	saxophone	piano	snare drum	flute
gong	tuba	piccolo	glockenspiel	chimes
guitar				

String Family
1. _____
2. _____
3. _____
4. _____
5. _____
6. _____

Brass Family
1. _____
2. _____
3. _____
4. _____
5. _____

Woodwind Family
1. _____
2. _____
3. _____
4. _____
5. _____
6. _____

Percussion Family
1. _____
2. _____
3. _____
4. _____
5. _____
6. _____
7. _____
8. _____
9. _____

The original purchaser of *Adventures with the Orchestra* has permission to reproduce this page for use in his or her classroom.
©2016 Heritage Music Press, a division of The Lorenz Corporation. All rights reserved. www.lorenz.com

CAN CAN—PARACHUTE FUN

Materials
- Recording of *Can Can #4* from *Gaite Parisienne* by Jacques Offenbach (visit http://music4you. lorenz.com/orchestra.html to find a suggested recording)
- Can Can PowerPoint (CD)
- 12-foot (or larger) parachute
- Family Musical Moment (CD)

Objective: Students will analyze the musical form of this piece and demonstrate their understanding through movement responses with a parachute.

My students and I always speak our corny little joke before we do an activity with this piece: "You often hear Beethoven and you often hear Bach, but you don't often hear... Offenbach!" Then I assign "homework" to the students, instructing them to go home and tell their parents what piece we did today, what movement activity we used, who the composer was, and to then tell them our silly joke.

Before You Begin

12-foot parachutes work well if you intend to toss the 'chute into the air at the end. Even my large classes fit around them, although it's tight. 20-foot parachutes are great if you want to "go under the mountain" at the end. If your classes are small in size, the 12-foot parachute will also work for the mountain.

The parachute is a very motivational prop, loved by all of my K–5 students. Often in their excitement they get carried away, which can be quite dangerous with 35 children in the room. In order to keep everyone safe and *keep the focus on the music*, I am quite firm in my instructions. It's best if you review the parachute safety procedures and behavior expectations *before* allowing children to touch the parachute. Here are some set-up statements that work for me:

- No rough treatment of the parachute, or "out-of-control shaking." The 'chute could be damaged, and you could hurt the arms of the students near you.

- No running under the parachute, unless it is part of today's routine.

- If we "Go Under the Mountain" you are to raise the parachute, turn your body to face outwards – resetting your hands accordingly – take one step in under the parachute, and then duck down and pull the parachute over your head. Seal the outer edges of the parachute with your arms to keep the air in and the "mountain" inflated. *No one is allowed to leave the edges and run to the center of the parachute!*

- If we toss the parachute into the air at the end, you *must not chase it.* If we all chase it, there will be chaos and someone could be injured. Let the 'chute fly, and land, where it wants. If that is on your head, you must stand still like a colorful, little ghost until I come and get the parachute off of you. (In one lesson years ago, a second grade teacher was in the room waiting to pick up her children, and the parachute floated off like a big jellyfish, landing right on her head! The children all fell on the floor laughing.)

- I promised our administration and your parents that I would keep you safe today, and so I promise *you* that if you are being dangerous during our parachute activity I will remove you from the lesson. This is my promise to you and the other students who deserve to be safe.

Directions:

1. Display and discuss the form chart (in the PowerPoint) with the children. Ask for the definition of *Introduction* and *Coda*. Question students as to which large sections occur more than one time.

2. Discuss the movement words for each section.

3. Demonstrate each movement while moving in a circular fashion, pretending to hold the parachute.

4. If you wish, click to the next slide in the PowerPoint, which shows the timings for the activity.

Introduction
Children are turned to the right in the circle, holding parachute with only the left hand, ducked over a little (not squatting down) in what we call "Sneaky Feet" position. When the music begins (and it is *very* soft and difficult to hear!) they begin to tiptoe while ducked down. Over the course of the eight-measure ($\frac{4}{4}$) Introduction they tiptoe faster and faster, raising their bodies up. By the eighth measure they will be fully upright in a quick jog.

A section (0:12)
Students quickly move into "Pony Trots", with their knees coming up high like a horse. Instruct them to jog, rather than running or galloping. A few beats before the B Section begins, instruct children to face the center and put two hands on the parachute.

B Section (0:24)
Match the musical high and low accented notes by moving the parachute up and down accordingly. My cue words are "High, then low, now shaky-shaky-shaky-shake." This happens four times.

C Section (0:36)
Large shakes to the beat.

This part of the music is so fun for the children (it's the theme they are all familiar with) that they scream and jump up and down while they're shaking the 'chute. Hooray for music class and the chance for children to express themselves *so* enthusiastically!

C Section Repeats (0:47)
Change from 'chutes shakes to The Washing Machine. Children move the parachute from left to right to the beat, like the agitator movement in a washing machine. Hopefully all hands will go the same direction and it gives a very cool visual effect with the parachute.

A Section Repeats (1:00)

Coda (1:10)
Facing the center, shake the parachute to the accented notes (half, half, quarter, quarter, quarter, quarter), pause the movement and get ready to toss the chute in the air on the last note, or "go under the mountain."

If tossing the 'chute:
Students bend over with the parachute at their knees. Upon the teacher's cue ("1-2-3-toss!") they toss the 'chute into air on the last note. Remind them to stay in place in the circle formation and let the 'chute fly where it may.

If "going under the mountain":
Students will raise the parachute, turning their bodies to face outwards, and resetting their hands accordingly. They will take one step in under the parachute, and then duck down and pull the parachute over their heads. They should seal the outer edges of the parachute with their arms to keep the air in and the "mountain" inflated. *And, for safety's sake, no one should leave the edges and run to the center of the parachute!*

5. Send home a Family Musical Moment strip with each student.

FAMILY MUSICAL MOMENT

Today in music class, we listened to the "Can Can" composed by Jaques Offenbach. Our instructional focus included form and steady beat. We activated the lesson with a parachute routine. Share a musical moment with your child by downloading this exciting piece of music and listening to it together. To download the recording we used, along with other wonderful recordings from NAXOS and its affiliate labels, visit music4you.lorenz.com/orchestra.html.

OVERTURE FROM WILLIAM TELL

by Gioachino Rossini

Materials
- Recording of the overture from Rossini's opera
  William Tell
  (Visit **http://music4you.lorenz.com/orchestra.html**
  to find a suggested recording.)
- Form Chart (CD)
- Stick Horses
- Family Musical Moment (CD)

Objective: Students will demonstrate their awareness of form while riding stick horses to a legendary musical work.

One day a girl came up to me and she said, "Dr. a., do you know what my favorite music is? William Tell. I love that music. I had a sleepover at my house this weekend with my friend and we painted on the ceiling with flashlights to William Tell." What a wonderful thing to hear from a student. Many of my students don't grow up hearing classical music in their homes, but that doesn't mean they don't enjoy it once they get to know it. They certainly certainly can't pick something as their favorite if they were never exposed to it! They just need a chance to hear it and interact with it in a child-friendly way. Who knows—they may pick their "favorite music" over more time with their electronics.

Before You Begin
This lesson works best if you have a stick horse for every student. I like the horses with the fuzzy heads that you can buy at discount stores, as well as the noodle-ponies that are shown on the internet. You can also make your own with two poster board horse heads, one taped to each side of a yardstick. The first time I made a set of stick horses, I covered the poster board in colorful wrapping paper of all different different designs. They sure were some cute horsies!

Directions:
1. Use the form visual to describe the form of this music. Talk about how the students will move the same way every time they hear the A music. Play the music, pointing to each section it plays.

2. Arrange your students in circles, leaving enough free space for each circle to move without bumping into others. You can put a circle inside of another circle to maximize space.

3. Give a horse to each student.

4. Practice each step of the routine below without using the music.

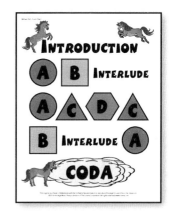

Introduction
Pawing ground, smoothing mane, flexing muscles, "Neigh…"

A Section (0:14)
Trotting to the right around the circle, heads up high on measure 4, then turn. Trot to the left four measures.

B Section (0:26)
Step into circle 4 beats, look at all your horsey friends.
Step back out of circle 4 beats, look at your rider.
Repeat

Interlude (0:39)
Pawing ground, smoothing mane, flexing muscles, "Neigh…"

Repeat A Section (0:45)

C Section (0:58)
Staying in place in the circle, leap on accented notes. Kick up heels while turning in place. (I call these "silly circles".)
Repeat

D Section (1:10)
Eat snacks from rider's pocket, then drink water. 8 beats each, 4 times.

Repeat C Section (1:32)
Repeat B Section (1:45)
Repeat Interlude (1:57)
Repeat A Section (2:03)

Coda
2:15—Leap over fence, then gallop freely through pasture.
2:22—Freeze! Look fearful. "Uh-oh! Did I hear coyotes?"
2:25—On each of four big chords, raise horse heads high to check north, south, east, and west.
2:32—Cheer! "No coyotes! Yay! Neigh…" Bounce happily in place.
2:35—Gallop freely through pasture.
2:41—Freeze! Look fearful. "Uh-oh! Did I hear coyotes?"
2:44—On each of four big chords, raise horse heads high to check north, south, east, and west.
2:50—Cheer! "No coyotes! Yay! Neigh…" Bounce happily in place.
2:54—Bounce in place until the next theme starts.
3:00—Big four-beat "Neigh…"
3:02—Free gallop and leap throughout room, but begin to tire. At the end of the piece, yawn, stretch, sink down to sleep on the last note, then snore.

5. After practicing all of the movements, play the music and call out directions to keep students moving with the music. The movements will fit so naturally with the sounds that you may not need to tell them every step.

6. Practice a few times until students have become independent with the movements.

7. Give your students a Family Musical Moment strip as they leave.

FAMILY MUSICAL MOMENT
Today in music class we listened to "Overture" from the opera *William Tell* by Gioachino Rossini. Our instructional focus included form with repeating sections like this one (ABACDCBA). We activated the lesson with stick horses. Share a musical moment with your child by downloading this exciting piece of music and listening to it together. To download the recording we used along with other wonderful recordings from NAXOS and its affiliate labels, visit **music4you.lorenz.com/orchestra.html**.

MARCH FROM THE NUTCRACKER

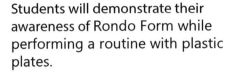

Materials
- Recording of the "March" from *The Nutcracker* (For a suggested recording, go to **http://music4you.lorenz.com/orchestra.html**)
- Plastic plates (two per student, with a few extra in case they break) *
- Form Chart (CD)
- Family Musical Moment (CD)

Objective
Students will demonstrate their awareness of Rondo Form while performing a routine with plastic plates.

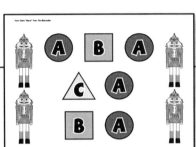

> *I use this wonderful piece throughout the year. It is fabuolous for teaching form, and the children always recognize the melodies. My little ones will often shout, "I've heard that music! I love that music!" So don't feel limited to using this piece just in the month of December.*
>
> *This activity began its life as a classroom lesson on rondo form. It then became an ensemble performance piece due to student demand. The children loved this activity, and their parents just ate it up at the concert. Most of the families had never heard of guided-listening lessons, so it was a wonderful opportunity to share how these types of activites are an important part of my curriculum to focus on music analysis.*

Directions:
1. Show children a visual of the form of the "March". First draw each shape below, then label each shape with a letter. Or you can use the form chart found on the CD.

2. Listen to the whole piece once, helping students to discover the rondo form. Note that the A section has two distinct parts: one that has a marching feel, followed by a section that sounds like galloping music. Those two parts then repeat, making the A section rather long.

3. To prepare for using the plates, listen to the recording again and lead your students to perform the following hand motions on their laps for each section, pretending they are holding plates: Pat laps, clap plates together, raise plates to sides of face, and clap plates together.

4. Arrange the children on risers (or seated in the classroom chairs or on the floor) and divide the students into three groups. Distribute red plates (or any color you choose) to the group on the left, white plates to the group in the middle, and green plates to the group on the right. Have the children hold their plates with their thumbs against the back of the plate and their fingers extending over the rim and flat bottom of the plate. To begin, all students should hold their plates in a starting position. We use "mouse ears' – holding the plates against our heads and above our ears, so we look like Mickey Mouse. Perform the movements to the music as follows, providing verbal cues as needed:

*I use eight-inch plastic plates. Paper plates are a possibility, but I prefer the durability and percussive sound of the plastic. The eight-inch size looks the best on stage, although if you are working with very young children you might consider the six-inch size. Red, green, and white plates make for a festive presentation during the holidays. Or pick any three colors for another time of year.

A Section: *all plates*
Listen to the first two measures of the A section to hear the beat. Move the plates to the music following this pattern: Pat plates on lap, clap plates together, hold out to sides by face, and clap plates together. Repeat this sequence four times. Then wave the plates from right to left to a half-note beat. Change the waving to a quarter-note beat to match the music. This works out to be four half-note waves and seven quarter-note waves. Repeat the entire sequence without resting during the first two measures.

B Section: *red plates only*
Pat the bottom of plates together – alternating with the right plate on top, then the left, like patting out a tortilla – eight times. We call these "taco claps". Next, pat alternating eighth notes on laps. Repeat both parts.

A Section: *all plates*
All plates repeat the A section but do not rest during the first two measures. The pattern/movements should start immediately with the return of the A section.

C Section: *white plates only*
Wave the plates upward in a wiggly motion for four beats, then back down in the same fashion. We call this "wiggly dots". Next, have the students fan themselves with the plates while leaning to their right for four beats, then to their left for four beats. Repeat both parts.

A Section: *all plates*
All plates repeat the A section but do not rest during the first two measures. The pattern/movements should start immediately with the return of the A section.

Second B Section: *green plates only*
Brush the bottoms of the plates together in large, brushing motions for eight beats. Then perform an eight-beat drum roll on laps with the plates.

Final A Section: *all plates*
Pat plates on lap, clap plates together, hold out above heads in a V, and clap plates together. Repeat this sequence four times. Then wave the plates from right to left to a half-note beat. Change the waving to a quarter-note beat to match the music. (As before, this works out to be four half-note waves and seven quarter-note waves.)

Repeat the entire sequence, but on the last section of the half-note and quarter-note waves, change the last four beats of the piece to: clap, clap, clap, up. The plates should be raised up above the head (arms in a V) to freeze on the final note. We life to put both plates together and "tip our hats" to the audience at the end.

5. Congratulate your students on a job well done and send them home with a Family Musical Moment Listening Strip.

FAMILY MUSICAL MOMENT
Today in music class, we listened to the "March" from the ballet *The Nutcracker*, composed by Pyotr Ilyich Tchaikovsky. Our instructional focus included rondo form and steady beat. We activated the lesson with plastic plates. Share a musical moment with your child by downloading this exciting piece of music and listening to it together. To download the recording we used, along with other wonderful recordings from NAXOS and its affiliate labels, visit **music4you.lorenz.com/orchestra.html**.

TREPAK "RUSSIAN DANCE" FROM THE NUTCRACKER

Materials
- Form Chart (CD)
- Recording of "Trepak" from *The Nutcracker Suite* by Pyotr Ilyich Tchaikovsky
  (Visit **http://music4you.lorenz.com/orchestra.html** for a suggested recording.)
- Ribbon wands or strips of silky ribbon (cut into three-foot lengths)
- Family Musical Moment (CD)

Objective: Students will analyze the form of this piece and demonstrate their understanding via movement with ribbon streamers.

Directions:

1. Display the Form Chart. Ask students to hypothesize what this form might sound like.

2. Survey the class to discover which children have heard of *The Nutcracker Ballet*. Explain that the music they are about to hear is the "Russian Dance" or "Trepak" from this famous ballet.

3. With the children seated, play the recording while leading the class in hand motions that mimic the movement routine described in step 5.

4. Distribute the ribbon wands and ask the children to spread out throughout the room.

5. Practice each step of the routine outlined below with the streamers.

A Section
- Wave the ribbon up and down quickly; repeat
- Turn in place while waving the ribbon (turning flourishes)
- Repeat

Second A Section
- Jump and move the ribbon up and down quickly; repeat
- Turning flourishes
- Repeat

B Section
- Wave the ribbon back and forth while pointing it downward for eight beats (wash the floor)
- Wave the ribbon back and forth while pointing it upward for eight beats (wash the windows)
- Repeat

Interlude
- Wave the ribbon up to one side quickly, then to the other
- Repeat, matching the rhythm of the music

A Section
- Wave the ribbon up and down quickly; repeat
- Turning flourishes
- Repeat

Coda
- Wash the floor for eight beats, then wash the windows for eight beats
- Turning flourishes for six beats
- Jump and finish with the ribbons up and arms out above head

6. Play the recording and perform the routine.

7. If you wish, give your students a Family Musical Moment note as they leave so that they can find the music online or purchase a CD.

FAMILY MUSICAL MOMENT
Today in music class we listened to "Trepak" from the ballet *The Nutcracker* composed by Pyotr Ilyich Tchaikovsky. Our instructional focus included AABA Form. We activated the lesson with ribbon wands. Share a musical moment with your child by downloading this exciting piece of music and listening to it together. To download the recording we used along with other wonderful recordings from NAXOS and its affiliate labels, visit **music4you.lorenz.com/orchestra.html**.

RONDO ALLA TURCA

Piano Sonata No. 11 in A Major, K. 331, by Wolfgang Amadeus Mozart

Materials
- Recording of *Rondo Alla Turca*
  (Visit **http://music4you.lorenz.com/orchestra.html**
  for a suggested recording, or search a streaming
  service for a performance by Vladimir Horowitz.)
- Animal responders (CD; see assembly directions below)
- Zip-top bags (one per student)
- Popsicle sticks (four per student)
- Form chart (CD)
- Mozart biography (CD)
- Mozart mix-up worksheet (CD)
- Family Musical Moment strip (CD)

Objective: Students will learn
about Mozart and his career
as a composer, and then bring
this piece to life using animal
responders.

Before You Begin
Print the animal responder pages from the CD on different colors of card stock for each animal.
Laminate the pages, then cut out the individual animal pieces. Tape each animal to a popsicle stick and
place one of each animal (four responders total) into a zip-top bag. Create enough sets so that every
student in your largest class has his or her own set.

Lesson
1. **Write** "SRPOCMEO" on the board and call on a student to unscramble this word that
   means a musical career (composer). Ask students to share the names of any composers
   they know. Display *Mozart Mix-up* on overhead transparency, projected via your computer,
   or in poster form.

2. **Facilitate** the *Mozart Mix-up* activity, leading students through each question and the answers
   that must be decoded.

3. **Explain** that today's featured listening piece is a virtuosic work that will be played on the
   piano. (Encourage predictions of what "virtuosic" means.) Each melody will be represented
   by a critter. The A section snakes upward, thus the snake. The B section is very vigorous and
   marked by a strong steady beat, like a galloping horse. The C section is very busy, reminding
   us of a bee. The Coda has numerous fluttery passages, like the fluttering of birds' wings.
   Display the form chart. Encourage students to always be looking up and checking to see
   where in the form they are as the pieces plays. Remember, "Good musicians always think
   ahead, look ahead, and most importantly, listen ahead."

4. **Distribute** one responder pack to each student. Have them check their package to make sure
   they have four pieces: A/Snake, B/Horse, C/Bee, and Coda/Bird.

Responder Activity
Remind the students that all guided listening is done in silence, and that they will need to watch the
instructor to be sure and match the beat or melodic direction of the sections. The teacher then starts
the recording and leads the students through the motions below, using the responder that matches
each musical section.

A Section (Snakes): Starting low in front of you, snake or weave the responder upwards for two measures, matching the piano music, and then move the snake back and forth (left to right) to the beat for two measures.
Repeat. (8 measures)

Tap the snake on the palm of your hand for four measures. (4 measures)

Snake the responder upwards for two measures. Move the snake back and forth to the beat for two measures.
(4 measures)

Tap the snake on the palm of your hand for four measures. (4 measures)

Snake the responder upwards for two measures. Move the snake back and forth to the beat for two measures.
(4 measures)

B Section (Horses): "Gallop" the horse responders back and forth in front of you.

C Section (Bees): Move the bees to match the contour of the melody throughout this *long* section. As the melody goes on for a length of time, start looking exhausted. Sigh occasionally and prop up your arm (at the elbow) with other hand. This little bit of silliness really illustrates the character of this melody. Busy, busy, busy! As the students begin to wear out, jokingly tell them that their job is easy compared to the workout that the piano player is getting!

B Section (Horses): Gallop the horse responders back and forth in front of you.

A Section (Snakes): Repeat as above.

B Section (Horses): Repeat as above.

Coda (Birds): Move the bird responders to show the contour of the melody, as well as the rhythmic elements. "Flutter" the responders during the twisting and turning parts. "Fly" the birds to a landing on other hand (I call this "their favorite tree branch") on the last note. Have the birdies take a bow to finish.

5. Send a Family Musical Moment strip home with each student.

FAMILY MUSICAL MOMENT
Today in music class we listened to *Rondo Alla Turca* composed by Wolfgang Amadeus Mozart. Our instructional goals included Form and Melodic Direction. We activated the lesson with Animal Responders. Share a musical moment with your child by downloading this exciting piece of music and listening to it together. To download the recording we used along with other wonderful recordings from NAXOS and its affiliate labels, visit **http://music4you.lorenz.com/orchestra.html**.

WHAT'S A WEBVISIT?

Extend the walls of your music classroom by taking your students on WebVisits. A WebVisit is simply a class visit to an educational website. There are a multitude of exciting destinations on the internet and the knowledge to be gained is often not available to our children via our existing classroom resources.

You will need a computer with internet access in order to take WebVisits. A projector or large monitor will enhance the experience, but WebVisits can still be successful if the ideal equipment is not available. I have even taken the class on WebVisits with students gathered together on the floor in front of my small computer screen. While the situation was not ideal, the material was still interesting and informative, and children enjoyed the experience. Don't forget the school's computer lab! If your school has one, gaining access may be as easy as asking for a time to use it. Then, these WebVisits could be done with each child at his or her own computer as you guide from a main station.

I will often choose an informative site on the internet and visit it for a number of consecutive lessons, each time exploring a different component of the Web site. The visits are usually about 10 minutes in length, leaving plenty of time in the lesson for other activities. I often add a school/home connection component to the lesson by sending home a WebVisit Exploration Page for students and their families to do together. It is motivational to offer extra credit to students who complete the worksheet with a parent, and return it (signed) to the music room. The extra credit might be in the form of a grade enhancement, or you could consider giving school incentives, music stickers or some other such reward. If students are allowed to work on their own in the computer lab during the school week, perhaps you could have a number of WebVisit Exploration Pages available there for independent study.

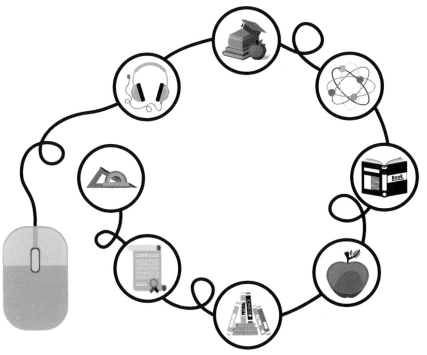

On the following pages, you'll find a wealth of detailed WebVisits, as well as suggestions for creating your own. There's no shortage of amazing (and often otherwise out-of-reach) musical experiences that can be found on the World Wide Web. Take advantage of it!

All of the websites used in this book are listed on the Clickable URL Index found on the CD. Use this PDF to quickly navigate to each site, instead of spending your precious planning time trying to type a complicated URL correctly.

THE NEW YORK PHILHARMONIC KIDZONE!

www.nyphilkids.org

Materials
- Computer with internet access
- Projector or interactive board (optional)
- Family WebVisit (CD)

WebVisit #1

Choose an exciting orchestral piece to play as Entrance Music while your students enter the classroom. (See suggestions on page 4. Be sure to tell the students the title and composer of the piece.) Begin the WebVisit with the Kidzone Main Stage page on the screen. Move your cursor over the sections of the site, calling on children to read the words that are displayed—game room, instrument storage room, dressing rooms, instrument lab, musicians' lounge, composition workshop, composers' gallery, newsstand.

Choose a student to come to the computer and use the mouse or touchpad to discover all the other segments of the website. The student will find that moving the cursor over each game tile will display a short description.

Resume control of the mouse and click on the instrument storage room. In this room the figure of a young boy walks through each instrument family storeroom as you drag the cursor right or left. When he enters a room, direct your students' attention to the cases and see if they can guess any of the instruments by their shape and size. Allow students to use a pointer and actually point to the case of their choice on the screen. Move the mouse over the case to see a picture of the instrument and its name. Continue by choosing more children to guess the instruments in each room. (See if your students can find the "controversial" instrument in the percussion storeroom. Although its strings are plucked, the harp functions as a member of the percussion section in most orchestral music, adding color and other flourishes.) You might also invite older students to click on the family name "picture" in each room. This will reveal a short article about that family that they can read to the class.

WebVisit #2

Choose another great piece of orchestral music for your Entrance Music. Begin the WebVisit with the Kidzone Main Stage page on the screen. Click on the dressing rooms. Use your mouse to walk the young girl to the left, entering the conductors' dressing rooms. You will see many conductors, including historical, current, and nontraditional choices. Choose a student to pick two conductors. Click on the photograph as well as the music stand to read all available information.

Walk the young girl back to the right until she enters the Soloists' dressing rooms. Pick any two to visit. There are many excellent choices, including soprano Kiri Te Kanawa, cellist Yo Yo Ma, The Boys Choir of Harlem, pianist Emanuel Ax, percussionist Evelyn Glennie, violinists Midori and Jascha Heifetz, and more.

WebVisit #3

While your new orchestral entrance music is playing, seat students in front of the computer monitor with the Kidzone Main Stage page displayed. Go to the game room. Choose a game to explore with your students. Consider having a number of children come to the computer and take turns playing the game. You could even form teams.

(When we play the Music Match Composers or Music Match Instruments, we alternate between boy and girl turns and keep score on the board.)

There are some very educational and fun choices, including:

- Percussion Showdown—a "Simon"-type game.
- Instrument Frenzy—a challenging "Tetris"- style game with dropping instruments that need to be sorted into families
- Orchestration Station—children can score a piece of music for instruments of their choice
- Make Your Own Instrument—children build instruments from found sounds.
- Music Match Composers (or Instruments)—"Concentration"-type match game

You will want to visit the game room a number of times to allow children to see the great choices in this area.

WebVisit #4

After fading out this lesson's orchestral entrance music, take children on a quick tour of some other great parts of this Web site. Begin at the Main Stage page and click on the composers' gallery. Ask a student to choose a composer to read about. Next, go back to the Main Stage and click on the Newsstand. Click on the papers of your choice and read the information with your students.

Suggested Entrance Music Choices

Rossini: Finale of the *William Tell Overture*

Khachaturian: "Sabre Dance," from *Gayane*

Holst: "Jupiter," from *The Planets*

Beethoven: Symphony No. 9

Offenbach: Can-Can, from *Gaite Parisienne*

Rimsky-Korsakov: Flight of the Bumblebee

Copland: "Hoedown," from *Rodeo*

Handel: Royal Fireworks Music

Haydn: Symphony No. 94 ("Surprise")

Tchaikovsky: "Trepak," from *Nutcracker*

Bizet: "Toreador Song," from *Carmen*

Extension Ideas

After you've completed these activities, reproduce the Family Connection page on the CD and send it home for the students to do with a family member. Consider offering extra credit of some kind for children who complete the WebVisit with a family member and return the signed form. This outstanding website includes other parts that you can explore in subsequent lessons, should you wish to extend the activity. You might also consider producing worksheets that students can fill out each week as you take your WebVisits.

Family WebVisit

After you've completed these activities, print the Family WebVisit page on the CD and send it home with students. The Family WebVisit will help students share what they've learned with their families, and give them a little more time to explore an educational website. I like to give extra credit when students bring back a completed form, signed by a family member.

THE VEGETABLE ORCHESTRA

www.gemueseorchester.org

www.youtube.com/watch?v=hpfYt7VRHuY

Materials
- Computer with projector or interactive board
- A large world map
- Family WebVisit (CD)

Objective: Students will categorize instruments into the four instrument families.
Students will evaluate a musical performance for expressiveness and ensemble interaction.

Some parts of this website don't work well with every browser. If you have problems, try using Google Chrome or Mozilla Firefox. Those worked well at the time of this printing. Or you could use the YouTube link instead. If you are concerned about inappropriate content on YouTube, or if your school blocks it, go to www.cleanvideosearch.com and paste in the YouTube URL.

Directions

1. Initiate a discussion about homemade instruments. Ask whether any of your students have created their own instruments, and if so, ask what they used to make them.

2. Explain that today's WebVisit will focus on "found sounds" that are quite unique!

3. Find Vienna, Austria on a map, explaining that the musicians you will "meet" are from Austria, and live in the capital city of Vienna. You may wish to go on and explain that historically Vienna was a center for the arts and that many famous composers lived and worked in Vienna, including Beethoven, Mozart, Haydn, Schubert, and Brahms.

4. Go to the Vegetable Orchestra website. Click on the "video" bar and watch the six-minute video. Your children will enjoy this unique video that begins with a trip to the Farmer's Market to test veggies for their acoustic qualities. Then it's off to the workshop where power tools help the musicians create Carrot Recorders, Calabash Congas, Eggplant Castanets, Red Pepper Mutes and more! As the concert portion of the video begins be sure the children are watching

   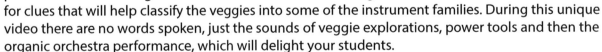

   for clues that will help classify the veggies into some of the instrument families. During this unique video there are no words spoken, just the sounds of veggie explorations, power tools and then the organic orchestra performance, which will delight your students.

5. Review the instrument families and the characteristics of each family. Ask your students whether they saw any woodwind veggies, percussion veggies, string veggies, or brass veggies. To answer this question, go to the "instruments" page in the "info" menu to view pictures of some of the instruments. If needed, watch short segments of the video clip again.

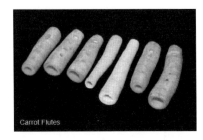
Carrot Flutes

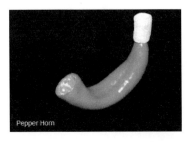
Pepper Horn

Pumpkin Drum

6. Discuss how the vegetable instruments produce sound and how the sound is amplified. For example, the cucumberphone has a mouthpiece like a trumpet and a mute, but it needs a microphone to amplify its sound.

7. Explore the "questions and answers" page to learn about the performers and their widely varied musical backgrounds; how the group began; and whether or not they are vegetarians.

8. Watch the performance sections of the video again. Comment on, and ask for discussion about the performance. Are the performers listening to one another? Is there a musical progression (form) to the piece? Does the piece have a steady beat throughout? Do they end together? Are there any soloists in the group?

9. Take a poll of the students' favorite vegetable instruments. Consider graphing this information for visual reinforcement.

10. Encourage your class to visit the website at home by distributing the The Vegetable Orchestra Family Connection sheet.

Extension Activities

Have older students think about and explore other instruments that can be made from renewable or recycled resources. They could even be assigned to make their own instruments. Collaborate with your art and science teachers.

Discuss how early instruments were made from natural resources. Have the class identify other cultures that have used vegetables to make instruments, such as Native Americans' use of gourds to make rattles or the shekere from West Africa.

Family WebVisit

After you've completed these activities, print the Family WebVisit page on the CD and send it home with students. The Family WebVisit will help students share what they've learned with their families, and give them a little more time to explore an educational website. I like to give extra credit when students bring back a completed form, signed by a family member.

STRING ENSEMBLE WEBVISITS

Materials
- Computer with internet access
- Projector or interactive board (optional)
- Family WebVisit (CD)

I do a selection of short, varied WebVisits for visual instruction of the string family. Most of the suggestions below are brief video excerpts, so that I can offer a nice selection of pieces in the short amount of time I have. Depending on the time available, you may choose to show the videos in their entirety. These videos are some that my students enjoy, consider motivational and will often revisit at home in their spare time.

The first four WebVisits, as well as WebVisit #7, feature a string quartet, which consists of two violinists, one viola player and a cello player. String quartets are widely seen as one of the most important forms of chamber music, and composers have written for this particular instrumentation for hundreds of years. Joseph Haydn was one of the most prominent composers of string quartets and, according to Oxford Scholarship Online, he wrote sixty-eight string quartets over a span of more than four decades!

WebVisit #1
Attaca Quartet, *Haydn: Op. 71, No. 1, Fourth Movement* (0:00-1:21)
http://attaccaquartet.com/video

WebVisit #2
Attaca Quartet, *Williams: Star Wars Theme* (0:00-1:06)
www.youtube.com/watch?v=9Rp4rLXbrDw

The Attaca Quartet formed at the Juilliard School in 2003, served as the Juilliard Graduate Resident String Quartet from 2011-2013 and was named the Quartet in Residence for the Metropolitan Museum of Art in New York City.

WebVisit #3
Art-Strings Quartet of NYC, *Vivaldi: Winter from the Four Seasons* (0:40)
www.youtube.com/watch?v=LcHh2qT-oS4

Formed in 1997, this quartet concertizes and provides music for special events including television commercials and shows. They have performed in some of the finest concert halls, including Carnegie Hall (NYC), Albert Hall (London) and Concertbegouw (Amsterdam). In addition to their event performances, they are all string teachers and members of local orchestras in the NY, NJ and Connecticut areas.

WebVisit #4
Joyous String Quartet, *Michael Jackson: Smooth Criminal* (1:29)
www.youtube.com/watch?v=4JJB7dCCQ7w

These very young players have lots of energy and excitement in their playing and my students love listening to them! Joyous String Quartet members have been performing together since they were four years old. Nine-year-old cellist Justin Yu appeared on the Ellen DeGeneres Show last September. The group has also made appearances in SBS Star King (Korea) and Hunan TV's Day Day Up show (China) recently. Based in Long Island New York, The Joyous Ensemble and Joyous Quartet perform 20 concerts a year around the world.

WebVisit #5
Black Violin (A String Duo), *A-Flat* (0:00-1:58)
www.youtube.com/watch?v=gEIVzWCRSg8

Black Violin is a hip hop duo from Florida. Kevin Sylvester (violin) goes by the stage name Kev Marcus, and Wilner Baptiste (viola) is known as Wil B. They met in high school, went to different colleges, then reconvened to create the musical group Black Violin. The duo plays a variety of music (relying heavily upon classical music), but are often categorized as hip hop because of the changes they make to the rhythm and beat. Mingling hip hop with classical sensibilities gives them a distinctive style.

WebVisit #6
Black Violin (A String Duo), *Brandenburg* (0:00-2:06)
www.youtube.com/watch?v=KCXVCpcopa8

Be sure to preview this video before using it in your classroom, to see if all of it is appropriate for your setting. My students love it, but to keep it short and, perhaps, non-controversial, I just show an excerpt (from 0:00-2:06). This shows the players' "genre-versatility" and the surprise on the audience's faces, and then the infectiousness of the players' musical treatment of this very famous work.

WebVisit #7
BOND, The Original Electric String Quartet; *Diablo* (0:00-1:25)
www.bondquartet.com
www.youtube.com/watch?v=NirRMrpbCFQ

Be sure that the picture on the website opening page is acceptable for your setting. I quickly move on to click the video below, or mute the projector until I click on the video. You can also go directly to YouTube link to see the same video.

Tania Davis (violin), Eos Counsell (violin), Elspeth Hanson (viola) and Gay-Yee Westerhoff (cello) are the members of BOND. They call themselves "the original electric string quartet." According to their website, the string quartet "has sold over 4 million albums worldwide, making it the best-selling string quartet of all time."

These highly educated musicians show a willingness to explore the joy of music without being limited by cultural tradition. They draw inspiration from different styles, such as folk, jazz, and Indian music, blending them together to discover the joy of music without being limited by culture or genre. You can see the pure energy as they play.

Family WebVisit
After you've completed these activities, print the Family WebVisit page on the CD and send it home with students. The Family WebVisit will help students share what they've learned with their families, and give them a little more time to explore an educational website. I like to give extra credit when students bring back a completed form, signed by a family member.

BRASS QUINTET WEBVISIT

Canadian Brass: Flight of the Bumblebee
www.youtube.com/watch?v=xZO5KTJTwhE

Materials
- Computer with internet access
- Projector or interactive board (optional)
- Family WebVisit (CD)

A brass quintet, the most familiar of brass ensembles, consists of two trumpets, French horn, trombone and tuba. This internationally acclaimed brass quintet, The Canadian Brass, is known for their virtuosic playing, imaginative arrangements, stage presence and rapport with their audiences. Their concerts include a wide variety of musical genres, as well as entertaining dialogue and theatrical effects.

Two fun facts for the students are (1) their concert attire consists of formal clothing and white running shoes, and (2) their instruments are all plated in 24 karat gold.

This 1:59 video is a wild ride for the brass players and the audience. The parts are extremely difficult and the tempo is vivace! The first trumpet player is playing on a piccolo trumpet, which is a smaller, higher version of a trumpet. The second trumpet player is playing on a trumpet of the most common size, the B-flat trumpet. In this WebVisit, my students are always captivated by the look of the tuba, with its dark bell. It is a black carbon fiber bell on a gold-plated tuba.

The Introduction allows the students to hear trills being played on each instrument, beginning with the tuba and moving in turn to the higher instruments. The famous bumblebee melody starts in the trumpet part at 0:25 and is passed around to the various instruments. At 1:08, note the amazing agility of the trombone player who plays the rapid melodic lines with a slide, not having the technical advantage of valves for fast passages. A bit of silliness in the Coda gives the children a laugh, as the piccolo trumpet player becomes a vocalist for the final note.

There are many videos that have been uploaded to YouTube by The Canadian Brass. In addition to *Flight of the Bumblebee*, your students would also enjoy *Toccata and Fugue in d minor* as well as *Amazing Grace*, which starts with a bluesy cornet solo and finishes in an exciting Dixieland style.

Family WebVisit
After you've completed these activities, print the Family WebVisit page on the CD and send it home with students. The Family WebVisit will help students share what they've learned with their families, and give them a little more time to explore an educational website. I like to give extra credit when students bring back a completed form, signed by a family member.

WOODWIND QUINTET (WIND QUINTET) WEBVISIT

Dvorak: American Quartet, 1st Movement, Allegro ma non Troppo (0:00-4:46, excerpt) performed by Amsterdam Woodwind Quintet
www.youtube.com/watch?v=ZnM6zozUwtC

Materials
- Computer with internet access
- Projector or interactive board (optional)
- Family WebVisit (CD)

A Wind Quintet consists of five instrumentalists playing flute, clarinet, oboe, bassoon and French horn. Lead the children in discovering which of these instruments is not a member of the woodwind family, but is a respected member of a Woodwind Quintet (French horn).

According to the International Music Foundation of Chicago, although the French horn is a brass instrument, its warm mellow sound blends well with woodwinds, which is why composers began writing it into woodwind quintet pieces years ago. This puts French Horn players into the unique and rewarding position of being able to perform in both Brass Quintets and Woodwind Quintets.

The excellent camera work in this video shows the technical facility of each player "up close and personal." Prepare the children to notice how each instrument gets its moments of playing the melody and then times of being accompaniment for the others. The melody is seamlessly passed between the members and they are careful to blend, sometimes being more "present", other times staying in the background and letting the other instruments' parts be featured.

Before the Introduction commences, point out to the students how the flautist begins the piece and "passes the part" on to the clarinet and horn players. The bassoonist then begins the main melody, which later is repeated by the flute player.

0:37 – Note the very expressive use of dynamics
1:57 – Draw attention to the *rallentando* leading into a beautiful clarinet solo.
2:46 – Nice solo statement from the French horn
3:07 – The drama builds
4:09 – Oboe solo
4:46 – Opening melody returns and I fade the volume and stop the video
(Another good exit point, if you choose to shorten the video, is at 3:20.)

Brief Video Spotlight: United States Army Woodwind Quintet
http://www.usarmyband.com/woodwind-quintet/the-us-army-woodwind-quintet.html#video

This 51-second video gives a nice overview of the woodwind quintet, while their music plays in the background.

Family WebVisit
After you've completed these activities, print the Family WebVisit page on the CD and send it home with students. The Family WebVisit will help students share what they've learned with their families, and give them a little more time to explore an educational website. I like to give extra credit when students bring back a completed form, signed by a family member.

PERCUSSION ENSEMBLE WEBVISITS

Materials
- Computer with internet access
- Projector or interactive board (optional)
- Family WebVisit (CD)

Eastman Percussion Ensemble, Burritt: *Fandago 13* **(5:45)**

www.youtube.com/watch?v=k7BerR_qbLw

My students are captivated by this exciting percussion ensemble video! I show a 3:18 excerpt to my primary students, but the intermediate students have no difficulty staying focused for the entire 5:45. The camera work is excellent, utilizing a lot of close-ups of the instruments and the performers' hands at work, with their multiple mallets and complex stickings.

Elicit details from the children about what they notice in the video. They are always fascinated by the resonator tubes beneath each bar of the mallet instruments (especially the *huge tubes* on the bass marimbas), which are so different than the wooden sound boxes on our Orff instruments.

Although pitched and non-pitched percussion are used throughout the video, the focus is on mallet percussion (pitched) from 0:00-1:26 and then the focus changes to non-pitched percussion from 1:27-3:18. The instruments utilized in this piece, composed by the Eastman Percussion Ensemble Director, include:

- Marimba
- Bass Marimba
- Xylophone
- Vibraphone
- Bell Tree
- Suspended Cymbal
- Crotales
- Concert Bass Drum
- Congas
- Bongos
- Toms
- Djembe
- Darbuka

Third Coast Percussion, Condon: *Fractalia* **(4:55)**

www.youtube.com/watch?v=bs_yMbao7IQ

This video's hauntingly beautiful melody showcases marimbas, with two players per instrument. There is a nice contrast between the mellow marimba sounds and bold, accented drum parts, which begin at 0:43. At 1:28 a crescendo leads into a drum feature by all four players, utilizing shell clicking as well as playing on the heads.

The Top Secret Drum Corps, Basel Switzerland at 2012 Edinburgh Military Tattoo (6:10)

www.youtube.com/watch?v=HW3QVLIK-kE

Your students will go straight home and show this WebVisit to their families! This amazing drum corps and color guard (flag team) from Basel, Switzerland will have the class enthralled for the entire six minutes and ten seconds. There is a nice mix of wide camera shots to showcase the precision marching patterns, and close-up shots to feature the extreme difficulty of the drummers' parts. Patterns, precision, practice, perfection, strength, complexity, challenge, endurance, focus, musicality, beauty...the adjectives are endless for this performance! Some fun highlights are:

0:40 – The *Wave* on the snare drums
2:14 – Flag poles are used as percussion instruments
3:30 – Dueling scene
5:05 – Drumheads light up when struck
5:25 –Accelerando Fun

The members of this non-military group are college students and men with day jobs such as factory workers, bankers, etc. They practice hundreds of days a year to perfect these extremely challenging routines!

The Top Secret Drum Corps, 2016 VIT (Virginia International Tattoo) (6:22)
www.youtube.com/watch?v=kd8UXijXtqM
(First U.S. appearance)

This is another great video of Top Secret, with two new twists for your students. At **3:38** the snare drummers pick up new pairs of sticks, which look like drumsticks, but are actually fifes! They become woodwind players to share "Scotland the Brave" with the audience. Then at **5:15** the children will enjoy seeing the flags turn into fireworks launchers.

The Hot Marimba Class 2011, Hampton: *S.D.G.* (3:26)
www.youtube.com/watch?v=Dxg8b4AtePg

Walt Hampton is the author of numerous books of arrangements for Zimbabwean-style marimba music. The pieces are unique, joyful and challenging and my students love them. In this video adults are performing one of his pieces.

'Baduku Marimba Band, *Mbube (The Lion Sleeps Tonight)* (4:10)
www.youtube.com/watch?v=ReT4HV9nlms

In this enjoyable video your students will see Mr. Hampton's student ensemble performing at an outdoor event. This group uses Zimbabwean-style marimbas, but there are many schools around the country playing these pieces on traditional Orff mallet percussion instruments. My student ensembles feature a Walt Hampton piece in each spring concert, adding non-pitched percussion interludes and recorder melodies.

Zimbabwe Marimba Band (2:20)
www.youtube.com/watch?v=AhHO8r2RigQ

This group's music is spirited and jubilant and my school children love this WebVisit. The brilliant use of dynamics and "body English" makes for a fun-filled 2:20! If you enjoyed this, check YouTube for some of the Zimbabwe Schools marimba challenge competition videos.

Family WebVisit
After you've completed these activities, print the Family WebVisit page on the CD and send it home with students. The Family WebVisit will help students share what they've learned with their families, and give them a little more time to explore an educational website. I like to give extra credit when students bring back a completed form, signed by a family member.

SAXOPHONE ENSEMBLE WEBVISIT

The Nuclear Whales Saxophone Orchestra: Sousa: The Stars and Stripes Forever (0:00-2:09)
www.youtube.com/watch?v=MaqcZ_4ZssU

Materials
- Computer with internet access
- Projector or interactive board (optional)
- Family WebVisit (CD)

I am sure that you are shaking your head and wondering why I have included a saxophone family WebVisit when (1) saxophones are members of the woodwind family, due to their use of a reed, and (2) very few orchestral pieces include saxophone parts.

This lesson is your chance to, once and for all, help those children who are continually assuming that the saxophone is in the brass family because it is made of brass. I've met numerous teachers who thought the same thing, and it is a reasonable, although incorrect, assumption.

When Adolphe Sax invented the saxophone for the French military bands in the 1800s, the instrument was designed to be a bridge between the brass and woodwind families. He wanted to create an instrument that had the technical facility of a flute or clarinet, but the volume and forward-facing bell of a brass instrument.

Saxophones are major components of wind ensembles, bands, and jazz bands. However, they were invented after a large portion of the orchestra repertoire was composed, so their inclusion in orchestras is minimal. Still, there are a number of orchestral works in which saxophones play a significant role, including:

Leonard Bernstein: *West Side Story*
George Bizet: *L'Arlésienne Suite Nos. 1 & 2*
George Gershwin: *American in Paris, Porgy & Bess, Rhapsody in Blue*
Modest Mussorgsky/arr. Ravel: *Pictures at an Exhibition: The Old Castle*
Sergei Prokofiev: *Romeo & Juliet*
Sergei Rachmaninoff: *Symphonic Dances op. 45*
Maurice Ravel: *Bolero*

This WebVisit features a saxophone choir, specifically, a sextet. Because of the *instrument-family-confusion* associated with saxophones, i like to do a saxophone-specific WebVisit and take the time to address the children's misperceptions.

The Musicians
The Nuclear Whales are a group of six American saxophonists based in California. Their instruments have a *very* wide range, utilizing sopranino, soprano, alto, tenor, bass and contrabass saxophones. The contrabass is affectionately known to my students as "The Big Beast" and it never fails to bring a dropped jaw, then a smile to their faces. It's quite an unusual and powerful sound!

Video Overview
In addition to their amazing range of instruments and superb musicianship, the Nuclear Whales love to infuse their performances with humor, choreography and props. This WebVisit is based on Sousa's *The Stars and Stripes Forever* and is a lot of good music and fun for the kiddos, due to the great playing, the contrabass features, and the sopranino player's "majorette" choreography, complete with instrument twirling. My students are also impressed with the fact that this group, like many professional chamber groups, have their music memorized.

The Sousa segment (0:00-2:09) is just the right length for young learners, but if you wish to go a little further in the video, the second piece is a lot of fun for children to see, featuring the amazing musical work *Also Sprach Zarathustra*. Although it's not as familiar to our students as to trained musicians, they will still enjoy the "twinkling stars" (flashlights on the player's heads) and the contrabass player miming an astronaut floating through space. It will help the children if you explain that this very famous orchestra work by Richard Strauss was used as the opening theme to a movie about space entitled *2001: A Space Odyssey*.

Additional Video Suggestions
Other saxophone ensemble videos your students might enjoy include:

- San Francisco Saxophone Quartet: Handel: "Hornpipe" from the *Water Music Suite in D*

- The Fairer Sax Quartet (4 females): Mancini: *Pink Panther*

- The National Saxophone Choir of Great Britain: *Bohemian Rhapsody* and Bach: *Toccata*

Family WebVisit
After you've completed these activities, print the Family WebVisit page on the CD and send it home with students. The Family WebVisit will help students share what they've learned with their families, and give them a little more time to explore an educational website. I like to give extra credit when students bring back a completed form, signed by a family member.

DESIGN YOUR OWN WEBVISIT

Consider taking your students on frequent WebVisits in music class. There are many outstanding websites to visit, with an extraordinary amount of educational material to be discovered. The orchestra-focused sites recommended below are all visually appealing with a multitude of valuable components such as instrument games, interviews with conductors, composers, and performers, music encyclopedias, coloring contests, music theory lessons, areas to design musical instruments, assistance in composing music, concert announcements, and much more.

Recommended Websites

DSO Kids (sponsored by the Dallas Symphony) has various features introducing the orchestra, as well as games.

www.dsokids.com

SFSKIDS (sponsored by the San Francisco Symphony) has interactive lessons that teach kids about the orchestra.

www.sfskids.org

BSO Kids (sponsored by the Boston Symphony) has musical games children can play.
www.bso.org/brands/bso/education-community/children-families/bso-kids.aspx

Classics for Kids has information about classical music and composers.

www.classicsforkids.com

From the Top features kids who play classical instruments.

www.fromthetop.org

Extension Activity

See if an orchestra in your area has an interactive website for kids. Or better yet, find out whether they have outreach programs that either bring musicians to your school or sponsor educational performances that your students can attend during the school day.